The Ministry of Ushering

The Ministry of Ushering

by

Mark R. Moore

Beacon Hill Press of Kansas City
Kansas City, Missouri

To those faithful stewards,

the ushers,

whose careful service
makes worship meaningful and enjoyable

Contents

Contents

Foreword

The pastor of a famous large city church was asked one time how he could account for the fact that great crowds thronged his services. His answer was this—"My ushers." He meant that the ushering corps of his church gave that first attractive impression to visitors that made them want to return. Long before they heard the preacher or the choir, they met the ushers and were well impressed.

We have for many years been concentrating, and correctly so, on improving the teaching in our Sunday School classes; and we have tried to insure strong, interesting preaching. But in all too many cases we have been slow to train our ushers. Why should we not also have trained ushers?

Mark R. Moore has given us in *The Ministry of Ushering* a splendid and adequate guide for ushers in any evangelical church. This book deals with all the phases of ushering, even ushering around the altar in revival services and during Communion.

The author has had a deep concern at this point for many years; the book simmered long upon the fires of his own heart.

I commend the author for having a burden for so vital a ministry. I endorse his book, for it is an answer to a great and growing need.

NORMAN R. OKE

Preface

This book is intended to fulfill a threefold purpose: (1) stimulate a deeper concern for church ushering, (2) provide a training manual for those contemplating serving as ushers, and (3) furnish a reading book on ushering so that ushers can refresh their minds periodically on their duties.

As a pastor, district superintendent, college president, and general church leader, I have observed that in churches where good ushering is practiced a friendlier atmosphere prevails and numerical growth is more apparent than where it is neglected. Good ushering is also conducive to spiritual growth. Such ushering, like any other Christian service that contributes to the well-being and advancement of the church, should be encouraged and fostered by the leaders of the church.

I will be pleased if this book is used as a means to help accomplish this end.

MARK R. MOORE

1 Why Usher?

The Value of Good Ushering

Any act that turns a person to Christ is a very important act. The good usher's contribution to the worship service in general and to the individual in particular is vital and far-reaching.

A visitor entered a large "First Church" in Dallas. He was a stranger within the gates. Many thoughts raced through his mind. He remembered old friends left behind and the close fellowship he had enjoyed in the friendly rural church back home. He wondered if these people could have the warm handclasp and the spirit of brotherly love. He even wondered, Will God be as near and as real to me here?

Once inside, the friendly usher greeted him in a congenial manner. He spoke, "Good morning! Smith is my name. What is yours?" The worshiper gave his name. The usher continued, "Mr. Jones, we are happy to have you in this service. Where would you like to sit?" The worshiper told him. Soon comfortably seated in an accessible pew, with hymnal and bulletin in hand, the visitor felt he was in the presence of friends. He had received a cordial welcome that fostered the spirit of worship. This usher had succeeded. The stranger worshiped God.

A pastor once told the writer that on two occasions visitors came into the services of his church. In both instances the ushers were busy, and the greeter was not at the door. The visitors searched for a seat. They came to one pew and started to sit down, only to be told, "This seat is reserved."

13

After encountering the same "This seat is reserved" three times in a single service, one visitor did not return.

"Be not forgetful to entertain strangers" (Heb. 13:2) is an impressive thought for the usher to keep in mind.

What Good Ushering Should Accomplish

There are many things accomplished for Christ and His Church through good ushering. Among them are:

Preparations for Worship. This includes meeting and seating the visitor and regular worshiper, providing hymnals and bulletins, and helping create an atmosphere of worship.

Maintain Order. During the intermission between the dismissal of one service and the beginning of a second service there is likely to be a period of confusion. The usher's wisdom and ability in handling the shifting groups can contribute much.

Promote Public Relations. The worshiper forms his first impressions of a congregation from his contact with those he meets in the vestibule. These impressions are important not only from the standpoint of the reputation of the church but also because they assist the worshiper in receiving the most from the service. These impressions are all the more important when the worshiper is a visitor. Successful is the usher who causes the worshiper to say, "I was a stranger, and ye took me in" (Matt. 25:35).

Ushers should be assigned to serve during Sunday School. New people need to know the location of classes, be introduced to a class host or hostess, and made comfortable and at home.

Give Courage and Faith. When Peter was sinking beneath the waves, Christ extended a hand and lifted him up to walk on the sea. A warm handclasp has, on occasion, influenced the course of life. Where should the needy go— except to God's house? The usher should bear in mind that

14

often the people are in need of the warmth, faith, and encouragement that come by a hearty hand grasp.

Lead a Person to Christ. The usher's method of greeting and seating a person who makes no profession of Christian experience may influence the person's receptivity to the message and have a definite bearing on his decision to accept or reject the invitation. Many of the world's leading evangelists have recognized that the usher is a key man and have given instructions regarding his responsibilities in the revival services.

THE PHILOSOPHY OF USHERING

Technically ushering means: to show into a room; introduce; escort, as into a room or to a seat; announce; herald or precede. Church ushering means vastly more. Ambrose R. Clark, dean of New York ushers, said, "Ushering is the art of making the church member and visitor feel comfortably at home and of lending spiritual dignity to the whole church service."

Another has said that ushering is the ability of a person to think of himself in the position of the worshiper, to anticipate the worshiper's needs, and to be able to assist him in the act of worship.

Andrew W. Blackwood said, "By promptness, courtesy, tact, and unobtrusiveness the usher helps the pastor and promotes worship."

The Primary Motive in Ushering

The primary motive in ushering should be the desire of the usher to serve God, his fellowman, and his church. When the invitation comes to a person to be an usher, he should feel that it is a sacred duty. Even more than a duty, he should look on it as a privilege. He should be honored that the pastor and board consider him to be a person of such fine

15

Christian character, ability, and judgment as to choose him to be "a doorkeeper in the house of my God" (Ps. 84:10).

THE DEVELOPMENT OF USHERING

Ushering dates back many years, but only recently have systematic study, organization, and training been employed to develop the art.

In the Secular World

Andrew Thomas Frain was called the king of ushers in the secular world. He deserved this title, for no one has done more to bring order to mass gatherings. As a 13-year-old youth he began his career at Wrigley Park in Chicago. Ushering was so poorly handled that about two-thirds of the patrons were improperly seated, and large sums were refunded to disappointed spectators after each game.

When Andy Frain was 18 years old Mr. Wrigley hired him at $15.00 per day to take charge of the ushering at the park. He did such a thorough job at Wrigley Field that he soon moved into other areas of service in ushering. He developed the largest professional ushering system in the world. Six years after he started his nationwide program of ushering his income exceeded $1 million. At the majority of mass gatherings such as games, conventions, large sales, fashionable weddings, and other social gatherings where professional ushers are employed, Andrew Frain's trained ushers moved the flow of people and made the occasion a time of enjoyment rather than of confusion.

Mr. Frain's secret of success was not to leave anything to chance. He secured blueprints of auditoriums or stadiums where he had to work and carefully studied the aisles, gates, doors, seating pattern, and parking lot. He used chalkboards and charts to familiarize his ushers with the situation. In addition, he used drills, regular exercises, and classes in personality studies to help prepare his ushers for their task. He made sure that they had thorough knowledge of the designation of tickets, location of exits, rest rooms, and other information necessary to being acceptable hosts. He also required that his ushers be honest and consistent in their dealings with the people. They were forbidden to accept bribes or show partiality.

In the Church

Before Andy Frain called attention to the deplorable ushering in the secular world, the church too had been working to correct errors, eliminate pitfalls, and develop ushering to a point of importance and service.

Ambrose R. Clark organized the first board of ushers in New York in 1897 in an endeavor to improve church ushering. His stated purpose and procedure of organization became the foundation for much of modern, organized church ushering.

Church Ushers' Association of New York

On January 10, 1914, ushers from 23 New York churches met and organized the Church Ushers' Association of New York. The purpose was to promote and develop a kindred Christian fellowship through ushering in the various Protestant churches represented in the association. These men felt that the exchange of ideas on church ushering and the service rendered by them were important factors in the religious work of the city. Soon the association had grown to include 62 churches representing 11 denominations.

Omaha School of Ushering

The municipal University of Omaha offered many courses in adult education. Dr. E. H. Hosman, director of adult education, originated a course in church ushering. The

17

first class graduated in 1944, and interest in the course grew. The founder gained national and international recognition for his contribution to church ushering. In addition to the courses held on the campus, the university offered correspondence courses, and Dr. Hosman conducted intensive classes on church ushering in various cities across the nation.

Books and Articles

The first published guide for church ushers was produced by the Church Ushers' Association of New York in 1914. Fleming H. Revell Company published a book titled *Church Usher's Manual,* by Willis O. Garrett, in 1924. This standard work still has wide acceptance.

Difference Between Ushering at Secular Events and Religious Services

We have seen that in the past 75 years there has been increased attention given to ushering both in the secular areas and in the realm of the church. Although both types of ushering have many things in common, they also have marked differences.

Ushering in stores, political conventions, places of amusement, and ball games is done primarily to serve and please the people. Often there may be an ulterior motive in view. For example, in relieving congestion during a store sale the flow of traffic is expedited, sales are increased, and as a result the company's profits are larger. The motive may be merely to direct persons to seats they purchased for the occasion or to fulfill a social function.

In the church, ushering is different. It may include most of the motives of secular ushering, but it includes much more. The church usher's job is one of promoting public relations and maintaining decency and order. In addition it is a service rendered to God and an act that plays an important part in the spiritual life of an individual.

The church usher is different. He deals with sacred things. He is a vital part of the greatest work on earth—Kingdom work. He is working under the King; "And whatsoever ye do, do it heartily, as to the Lord, and not unto men; knowing that of the Lord ye shall receive the reward of the inheritance: for ye serve the Lord Christ" (Col. 3:23-24).

Difference in Ushering in Various Churches

The same organization of ushers will not meet the need in every situation. It is obvious that there are differences in large and small churches. In the small church, members and friends are better acquainted; the worshipers' habits are more fixed; and the usher may be a bit more informal in discharging his duties. However, the small church service will be benefited by ushers who stay on the job and are ready to assist, although their services may not be needed as often as in the large church.

In the large church the worshiper often feels more alone. City life tends to create greater personality distances. Often the worshiper spends the week in the midst of rugged business activities, facing the competition of matter-of-fact commercialism, and is in real need of understanding and friendliness. It is a challenge to the usher of a large church to appraise the situation and rise to meet the need.

The occasion also calls for a different approach on the part of the usher. There is a distinct difference between ushering at a funeral and at an evangelistic service, or at the morning worship service and at a mass convention.

There is a place for the usher in each church and during each service. It is to the advantage of both the usher and the worshiper to sense the different needs and be able to meet them.

2 General Qualifications of the Usher

One business survey revealed the reason for business losses as follows: 1 percent of the customers died; 3 percent moved away; 5 percent found better prices; 9 percent changed stores for better treatment; 14 percent had a personal grievance; and 68 percent left because of the indifference of the clerks.

In a technical sense the church is not in commercial business, yet many have found that the same principles that help business also benefit the church. Indifference to the worshiper may eventually drive him away. No layman is in a more advantageous position to eliminate indifference than the usher. Much depends on him and his qualifications.

The major responsibility of ushering falls on a small group. Generally ushers serve admirably. But there are many members who have the qualifications, if they could be challenged and trained. Most any layperson with willingness to serve the Lord can, with study, prayer, and practice, become a good usher.

PERSONAL FAITH

The usher is an official representative of the church. He is a public-relations person. If he does not fully represent the church, he will bring reproach upon it. It is more advantageous to have an usher with lesser ability, in possession of an experience of grace and truly representing the standards of conduct of the church and with full confidence of the people, than to have one short of the standards although he has greater efficiency in other areas. The usher's position places him in the public eye, and the church is the loser if he fails to meet expectations.

The faith believed and taught by the followers of Christ is a vital personal experience with God through Christ. The usher should possess it.

Christ speaks of himself as "the way, the truth, and the life" (John 14:6). He also refers to himself as the Door. Those engaged in the business of pointing out the Door to others will be more effective by having entered the Door themselves. The usher of the church is a representative of Christ, and to truly represent Christ he must be Christlike.

The need for Christlikeness will arise. The manner in which things are done is often more important than the things themselves. Actions speak louder than words to most people. Frequently the usher should remind himself that people see and feel as well as hear. It is inevitable that occasions will arise that will try the soul of an usher. If, on such occasions, the usher becomes exasperated, harsh, or critical, he will do great damage to the cause of Christ. Even if an usher controls his speech, yet permits a carnal facial expression to discipline those involved in error, the results will be almost as damaging.

Courtesy, love, patience, long-suffering, and other Christlike traits come from the heart. One needs a Christlike heart to meet the problems with a Christlike spirit.

SHOULD A NON-CHRISTIAN USHER?

The question may arise, "What about a non-Christian

serving as an usher?" Two considerations prompt this question. The first is a need of ushers. Often there are not enough men within the smaller congregation, and a non-Christian could be used. The second reason is to help the individual by giving him a working interest in the church. Men who exemplify clean moral living could be helpful to the church, and the church in turn might help them if they were to serve as ushers. Because the usher is a representative of Christ, it is preferable that good Christian ushers be used. However, each local situation will have to be solved according to its own merit at the discretion of the local church leaders.

HEALTHY MENTAL ATTITUDE

The mental condition of the usher also affects his services. If he faces his task without the proper mental attitude, he may become a liability rather than an asset. If he feels that he is in the wrong place or that he is doing someone a favor or that the work is a burden, he is likely to fail. If he accepts the assignment as a sacred calling of Christ and considers it a privilege to serve God and the church, and that in his selection he has been honored, he is more likely to succeed. Blessed is the usher who lives by the meaning of Christ's words, "He that is greatest among you shall be your servant" (Matt. 23:11).

Proper Attitude Toward His Assignment

When the usher realizes that he was selected because of his character, willingness, judgment, and ability, it will be easier for him to sense the place of importance he holds. There is, of course, always the danger that he may feel too important. A good remedy for this mental attitude is to recognize that all spiritual ministry is under and through the Holy Spirit. He is the One who blesses service rendered and makes it effective. A feeling of dependence on Him will lead to the place of prayer and keep one humble in the Master's service.

The usher gives his service as unto God, but he does so by serving the people. By and large, people want and need loving service. They can detect sham and pretense. Insincere service is beneath the dignity of a good usher.

The petty annoyances that come to an usher are likely to influence his mental attitude if he does not have a clear vision and a steadfast faith that God will honor his efforts. He should remember that immediate results are not usually obvious and that appreciation is not always forthcoming.

The usher is the key man in developing an attitude of worship for and among the members of the congregation. The best-planned service can be ineffective if the ushering is bad. The usher's own spirit of reverence will make a contribution.

Loud talking, long conversations, or secret conferences with other ushers either before or during the service will hinder the atmosphere of worship.

Willingness to learn is another important factor in successful ushering. No two people are alike. It takes patience and effort to understand people. No two services are exactly alike either. An usher must learn to adapt himself to new situations. Only through careful study of people, readiness to adjust to circumstances, and determination to improve his technique will an usher reach the peak of his efficiency.

One of the most effective methods of learning is "on-the-job training." The workers themselves must recognize their own problems, and as far as possible all members of the group should meet together to solve their problems. In attempts to solve the problems, the emphasis should be upon the job rather than upon the person who is doing the job. This approach is significant. These principles should apply whether the meeting is a meeting held by the pastor or the head usher, or whether it is a series of meetings conducted in a training class.

When meetings are called, the usher should attend. There are many items that make regular meetings helpful to the usher. A planned book review on public relations or on meeting people is profitable. Talks from ministers and businessmen give inspiration and guidance. Roundtable discussions often bring to light the peculiar problems facing the usher, and many times a solution is found within the circle of the ushers themselves.

Willingness to share experiences and knowledge with others contributes to the success of the group. It is not enough just to share information with the other ushers, for there will be times when the entire task must be shared with new and inexperienced ushers. Readiness to receive others into the group and help them make the adjustments is of vital importance.

PROPER PRAYER LIFE

One of the dangers to those who deal with spiritual things is that holy things become commonplace. It is likewise true that those who are charged with the responsibility of conducting the service may become so involved with the mechanics that they miss the opportunity to receive help from God through the religious service. One of the best safeguards against this danger is to maintain a consistent prayer life.

Group Prayer

A good practice for the usher is to come several minutes before the other worshipers and engage in a few moments of devotional praying. God honors prayer, and those who hope to be the most effective in their service to God must spend

24

time in prayer. There are at least five things for which the usher should pray.

1. Pray that God will help him to be a radiant Christian example.

2. Pray that God will give him wisdom to discharge his duties in an acceptable manner.

3. Pray that God will bless his labors. Surely if God takes notice of a cup of cold water given in His name, He is interested in the service the usher renders in His house.

4. Pray for the worshipers—the visitors in particular.

5. Pray especially for all those who have a part in the service.

Maintain an Attitude of Prayer

The usher should always have a reverent, prayerful spirit. By praying more, he will not work less but he will accomplish vastly more. He can breathe a prayer as he works, for prayer is not all talking; it is partly listening to God. "Speak, Lord; for thy servant heareth" (1 Sam. 3:9-10) might well be the usher's constant innermost request.

Prayer the Best Antidote

Prayer drives away discouragement and builds up faith and zeal. It strengthens the usher and makes him more sensitive to his task. Prayer tends to eliminate carelessness and gives purpose to his assignment.

KNOWLEDGE OF BUILDING AND EQUIPMENT

The usher's skill will be determined in part by the knowledge that he has of the building, the seating space, and the people.

The Building

The usher's knowledge should include the location of fire escapes, how to regulate heating or cooling systems, how to adjust the windows, location of telephones, rest rooms, and other facilities. To illustrate this point: During a service the wind kept blowing the door of a classroom open and shut. The banging was distracting. A thoughtful usher went around the church, entered the educational unit, closed the window and door, thus putting an end to the noise. He did not stop there but gave a notation to the janitor to fix the latch on the door, so that it would catch firmly when closed.

He should have as much general knowledge about the heating plant, public-address system, building, lights, and equipment as possible. By all means he should know whom to contact quickly should problems arise with any of them beyond his knowledge and control.

Some problems are primarily the janitor's responsibility. There should be full and agreeable understanding on these points. Some congregations have it so arranged that the janitor's work is completed before the congregation arrives. The ushers then take complete charge and call on the janitor only in case of definite need. The ushers are the hosts during the public services, and the caretaker's work is done between services.

A comfortable temperature should be maintained at all times. The body temperature of people raises the room temperature, and moving air is cooler than still air.

Seating

To avoid the awkwardness and embarrassment of people being forced to stand in the aisle while the usher searches for seating space, he should know how many pews there are and how many persons can be seated comfortably on each pew.

After the usher has served for a while he will gain a general idea of how many will be in attendance. If he foresees that the auditorium will be only half filled, he should

26

try to seat the people comfortably together and toward the front. A scattered congregation creates problems for the speaker. Dr. W. H. Thompson, a psychologist, says a speaker begins to lose his congregation from the outer edges first. Disintegration begins there and then spreads over the remaining part of the audience.

3 Developing the Usher's Qualifications

IMPRESSIONS

The personal appearance of the usher is significant. It affects the dignity and decorum of the service, speaks for the church, impresses the worshiper, and has a definite bearing on the usher's own morale.

Too much stress cannot be placed upon the importance of the first impressions a newcomer receives as he enters the church. All areas of society have duly emphasized the significance of first meetings to the extent that we are convinced that first impressions are lasting impressions.

The usher should keep in mind that every service is a new experience to the regular worshiper and visitor alike, and it is up to him, as usher, to give a good impression. This means more than to look the part of a congenial and interested host. It means, be one.

Three Essentials

Go Easy. It is unwise to greet a worshiper too exuberantly. Too much vivaciousness appears superficial. One writer expressed the thought that exerting too much effort, rather than too little, is what drives others away. More than likely the worshiper is not in an attitude for such a lavish

28

greeting and does not desire to be the occasion or center of a scene. The usher should be natural, and then it will not be difficult to repeat the greeting over and over again.

Be Alive. This is not a contradiction of the above admonition. It is appalling for the usher to be passive, drab, and unconcerned. The deadpan expression and lifeless handclasp are as obnoxious as the superficial enthusiasm. The usher can be vigorously alive and yet naturally so. As such he is sure to be of great service to Christ and the church.

Be Neat. The physical appearance is most important. The usher is not a department-store model, and his attire should not smack of display. On the other hand his appearance should be in keeping with the high position he is filling. The usher should wear his clothes carefully, making sure his hair is well groomed and his shoes shined. His clothing should be pressed and his shirt fresh. The usher is expected to be clean in his person. The public will not excuse obnoxious body and breath odors. Excessive use of perfume is not suitable.

The usher's posture has a bearing on his appearance and carriage. He should keep both feet on the floor and stand erect rather than put his foot on a chair, permit his shoulders to droop, or lean against the wall. The important business at hand demands that he be at his assigned post, alert and ready for the appearance of a worshiper.

Many have found it advantageous to have something that distinguishes them as ushers. It may be an identification name badge, a flower in the buttonhole, uniform ties, or even suits as nearly alike as possible.

Rather than not have adult ushers, there are a number of smaller churches that use teen ushers. In most cases they have dress or armbands that distinguish them as ushers and usherettes. Some churches use high school and college youth on Sunday evening to replace adult ushers. With a good head usher supervising, this is excellent training and provides good ushering.

ADMIRABLE TRAITS

More and more pastors and churches are realizing that a skillful usher is one of a church's greatest assets. The usher's procedure in the discharge of his work will determine his usefulness.

Cooperation

The usher will receive many requests. If at all possible, he should comply with them. There will be requests for the usher to call cabs for the aged, to relay messages to friends, to be on the lookout for a father who has not attended the service but will drive up for the children about the time of the benediction. The effective usher will be considerate of each one.

People rush during the week. The ushers should not make them feel ill at ease as they spend a few minutes meeting and greeting friends in the vestibule at the close of the service. At the same time they should keep a passageway clear for those who wish to leave.

The usher should make it a rule to never argue with a worshiper. The usher may be right in ushering the worshiper to sit in a certain place, but it is better to give him the seat he desires, unless it is impossible.

Courtesy

Courtesy is one of the usher's greatest assets. If the person does not follow to the pew selected, the usher must not be discourteous. He must remember the slogan: "The customer is always right." On one occasion the worshiper stopped sooner than the usher had anticipated, whereupon the usher made gestures that suggested he was pulling his

30

hair. The good usher does not dramatize nor express disgust nor disappointment. In a situation like the above, he should return to the worshiper, present him with a bulletin, and continue his work, looking for other available seats or caring for some other phase of his work in order to pass off his own embarrassment.

He should treat all with equal courtesy. He should not be indifferent to rich or poor, and neither should he cater to one to the exclusion of the other.

In a midwestern city a doctor came into service late after being detained with hospital calls. The church was crowded. Although the head usher was seated in a chair near the rear entrance of the building, the doctor searched for several minutes for a seat unassisted. The pastor was chagrined. He had worked for several months to interest this doctor in attending church, and this was his first visit.

On another occasion a mother with several children came in. Their clothing bespoke meager means. She was forced to search several sections before finding seating space for the family. She left the service never to return. No doubt she felt she was not wanted, as no one provided a welcome.

The usher should gauge his steps to the speed of those he is seating. Often personal assistance to a worshiper will be appreciated. One wise usher conducted a blind woman to her seat, holding her arm as an old friend might do, with no suggestion that she might need help. When she was seated he placed the order of the service in her hands as he did with everyone else.

The church was crowded, and the ushers had brought several chairs and small benches into the auditorium in an effort to accommodate the people. As one usher passed a bench that protruded into the aisle, he suggested to the lady following him that she watch the corner of it. He merely stepped around it and, with a movement of his hand indicating the bench, said, "Watch this bench, please."

31

Friendliness

B. F. Sylvester, in his article "Sunday Morning Traffic Cops," told of a worshiper who entered one of New York's most fashionable churches and failed to remove his high silk hat. During the hush following the benediction one of the ushers asked the gentleman why he had kept his hat on during the service. To this question the man replied that he had been attending the church for 27 years and that he had bet his wife that he would make one of the ushers speak to him!

There are two extremes to be avoided: the one—the haughty, stiff, cold-shouldered, poker-faced type; the other—the too hale and hearty, happy-go-lucky, back-slapping type. One is so aloof and unfriendly as to be disgusting, while the other is so familiar as to be repulsive. The usher should be friendly in a normal manner—cordial, warmhearted, and kind. He should be friendly with all and familiar with none.

Resourcefulness

Many people develop habits and operate well in only one realm. The usher must be able to grasp a new situation and act in accordance with the need.

In Texas, during a preaching service, the pastor saw several papers blown from a table into an open gas heater in a Sunday School room to the rear of the auditorium. Since it was near some curtains, the building was in danger of catching fire. Without any explanation the minister publicly asked an usher to step into that particular room. The usher did so, extinguished the fire, and returned to participate in the worship. This usher saved a service and perhaps a building.

Ushers may have to use their ingenuity on other occasions. For example: The telephone rang in the minister's study. An usher saw that many of the 600 people were concerned and disturbed as it continued to ring. He found the janitor, unlocked the side door to the study, and answered the emergency call.

The usher will be called upon to perform many varied tasks. Among them will be passing out pledge cards, envelopes, revival announcements, and the like. There are a few simple rules for satisfactory coverage. One is to have a sufficient number of ushers. One Sunday morning six ushers were called to pass pledge cards to 800 worshipers. They had to work the main auditorium, balcony, and choir, and it took well over 10 minutes. With an adequate number of ushers, well stationed, they should have completed the task within 3 minutes. It is better to have too many ushers than too few.

Another rule for passing out items is to begin at the front of the congregation and work to the rear of the auditorium. It is advantageous to face the people. The usher should hold the item in his hand and present it at the slightest indication of desire. He should keep his eyes on the people, looking back once in a while to see if those just passed have changed their minds. He must not go too fast nor linger too long.

The usher's resourcefulness will be tested by various crises. Fifteen hundred persons were crowded into the church for the funeral of a prominent Omaha man who had lived in Lincoln, Nebr. The organist had played, and the minister was beginning his eulogy. The front of the church was so filled that the preacher could not see below the pulpit. The head usher was looking about to make sure that every detail had been looked after. It seemed that one had not. He left the sanctuary and went to the side of the pulpit, where, unobserved, he passed the minister this note: "We have no body!" The minister knew what to do too. He said a few more words and mentioned to the organist to play as if that were some new way of dividing the service.

Meanwhile the usher had found the Lincoln and Omaha morticians talking together in a corridor. Each was horrified to learn that the other had not taken care of getting the casket to the church. The head usher did not wait for them. He summoned several ushers, hurried to the nearby mortuary, got the casket, and carried it into the vestibule. Then the morticians moved the casket to the proper place in the church. The organist stopped playing and the service was resumed.

Promptness

If an usher is to serve well, he must be at his post on time. This means that he should be there at least 15 minutes before others arrive. He should take a bird's-eye view of the sanctuary and go through the checklist. The head usher should see that his colaborers are present in full force and be on guard against any oversight that might interfere with the smooth operation of the service.

Preparedness

The usher should anticipate needs and be ready for them. A sure way of success is for the usher to be ready for the routine or unexpected. Among some of the more important matters that may be routine are:

1. The pastor should be consulted prior to each service as to his desires regarding ushering. He might have plans to receive an extra offering, pass out missionary envelopes, make preparation for a dedication or baptism or other similar event.

2. The entrance should be checked to make sure that the caretaker has removed unsightly objects, shoveled off the snow, and in case of icy weather, spread salt or other suitable chemicals on the walks. God's house should be the cleanest building in town and present the most inviting entrance.

3. The doors should be checked to see that night latches are off, side doors are open, and fire exits clear.

4. Lights should be checked. Entrance and hall lights should be on as well as those in the rooms to be used. At night the outside entrance lights should be turned on about 30 minutes before the service. The light here should be bright enough to show the steps and entrance.

5. When hearing aids are provided they should be placed in the pew or in a location where the worshiper can get his own.

6. The telephone bell can be softened by checking with the telephone company. Phone jacks are convenient. The telephone should be silenced or moved from near the platform to the vestibule during the service.

Most of the above is the responsibility of the caretaker, but the usher should check to be sure things are in readiness for the service.

UNDERSTANDING THE CONGREGATION

The usher will have at least four types of people with which to deal.

The Regular Worshiper

Most folks have their likes and dislikes relative to a method of greeting and place to sit. With some it is more or less unconscious, while others are frank to express it. The reasons may be sensible and valid, but often they appear unreasonable.

The end-seater, who makes others climb over him, may be a claustrophobe (afraid to be closed in) and is not selfish in his desire. The middle-seater, who must sit away from the end, may be an agoraphobiac (afraid of open space). The same-seater, the person who has used the same pew for 30 years, would feel strange in another section. The immovable may have reasons not to change places. The family-seater just likes to have the family sit together as a unit. Each with his own desire—reasonable or seemingly unreasonable—has a right to his own opinions, and as the usher becomes aware of these spoken or unspoken requests, he should grant them.

The Visitor

It is wise to place the visitor in the best available pew, making certain meanwhile that he has a hymnbook and an order of the service. He must not be put off completely to himself nor crowded into too small a space. Generally he does not want to be too near the front nor too near the rear of the auditorium. The usher will give him his preference should he express one. If the visitor is seated too near the rear of the building he will be the first to leave, and the regular members miss the opportunity to make his acquaintance. Insofar as possible the usher should seat the newcomer near those who will put forth an effort to make him feel welcome.

The Mother with Small Children

There are several ways the usher can care for this group. Sometimes they are not welcomed and stay away altogether. This is harmful to the church and unfair to the mother and the child. Most churches provide nurseries, while others provide a soundproof nursery room at the back of the sanctuary, equipped with a loudspeaker. Here mothers may take care of their babies and still be a part of the service.

The usher's duty is to invite the mother to use the facilities the church provides, without offending her. If the church has not provided facilities or if the mother does not choose to use them, then the usher should seat her near the back where she may leave when necessary without personal embarrassment or undue disturbance to those nearby.

The Young People

The best policy is to have the entire family sit together. Assistance from the pastor through the bulletin and a sermon encouraging such a practice will do much to help solve the youth gang talk. If the family does not sit together, the usher should try to place the young people near some interested and responsible adult.

4 How to Usher

The usher is of fundamental importance in the worship service. He can mar or create the spirit of worship. Insincerity, looseness, lightness, and frivolity drive people away; but a sincere, heartwarming smile is pleasant and attractive. There are times when it requires effort to be pleasant, but it pays big dividends.

GREETING THE WORSHIPER

In many churches the hostess or host (often called "greeter") meets the people as they arrive. The importance of the greeter's function of establishing a contact between the visitor and the usher, and eventually the congregation and pastor, must not be overlooked. There are times when the usher and greeter are one and the same. If this is the case the usher should keep in mind the distinction between meeting and greeting of the visitor and that of seating the visitor.

Boards who are charged with the responsibility of selecting ushers many times overlook the possibility of having a lady serve as greeter or hostess. There are certain capable persons fitted for this task.

A minister in Great Falls, Mont., writes that a friendly, well-dressed, intelligent, middle-aged woman serves his church as greeter. She meets the visitors and presents them to the usher. She secures the name and address of each visitor, and at the close of the service she returns to the entrance and presents the visitors, by name, to the pastor.

Nearly everyone understands the necessity of a greeter in a large church. Even in smaller churches, where perhaps only one or two families visit on a Sunday, greeters can render a real service.

Seating the Worshiper

The head usher or greeter will be the first to meet the worshiper. This greeting should be with a natural smile and a friendly handshake—not a perpetual smile nor a bear grip nor a jellyfish handshake.

The head usher or greeter presents the worshiper to an usher, who in turn leads the person up the aisle to a seat or directs him to another usher located in the aisle. The transfer from one usher to another can be made at a distance if eye contact and acknowledgment of understanding are made between them.

The usher at the end of the pew where the worshiper is to be seated should face the worshiper as he makes his way up the aisle. The usher can place his hand on the back of the pew in front of the one where the worshiper is to be seated. When a pew is thus offered, seldom will a worshiper move elsewhere. The usher should remain beside the pew until the person has taken his seat.

As the usher moves about he should do it with dignity and poise. He should never cross the sanctuary between the minister and the congregation unless there is a dire emergency.

What to Give the Worshiper

The usher may keep the hymnals and open them to the correct page if the congregation is singing. When the people are arriving too fast for this, he can tell them the number as he hands them the hymnal. This is done in many smaller churches, and some large churches follow the plan. However, many churches prefer to have the hymnals in a rack on the back of the pew.

The usher will give the worshiper a bulletin. This is done, not at the door, but at the seat, so the worshiper will not be as likely to drift away from the usher on the way down the aisle. Care should be taken to present the bulletin with the face up.

If several classes meet in the auditorium during the Sunday School hour, sufficient number of ushers should begin at the front and work to the rear of the auditorium with bulletins for those who remain. Some find it advantageous to pass the bulletins before the Sunday School hour rather than just prior to the regular morning worship service.

When Not to Seat the Worshiper

By no means should the usher seat people during prayer, Bible reading, or a special song. The vestibule doors should be closed during these times to remove the likelihood of confusion. In the meantime, if a group gathers in the vestibule the usher should help them get into the spirit of the service. If it is during prayer he can, with bowed head, lead them to pray silently while waiting. If it is during the special song or Bible reading, he can listen and thus inspire reverence. As soon as possible, without appearing rushed, the usher should seat those who have waited.

When Not Engaged in Activities

When the usher is not busily engaged in the act of seating someone or caring for other specific responsibilities, he should participate in the worship service. It is important for the usher to preserve silence and dignity (else his work will be ineffectual). If he finds it necessary to talk, it should be done as inconspicuously as possible.

When assigned to a certain aisle the usher should stay there and not wander around the church nor hinder other ushers by visiting with them. Even as two ushers stand to-gether near the entrance waiting for the arrival of worship-ers they should not engage in joke telling or boisterous and distracting conduct.

Reserved Seats

If the auditorium is larger than the expected atten-dance, the usher is justified in blocking out certain sections. If there are those who want to enter this section, the usher should not argue but simply state that this section is re-served and move on to another area.

Even if the anticipated attendance is expected to fill the sanctuary to capacity, it is a wise practice to reserve the back pews for latecomers, mothers with small children, or place for ushers and collectors. This is particularly desirable if the church is located in a tourist area.

In some churches the regular worshipers choose their own seats and the ushers assist only the newcomers. Un-doubtedly the best results are secured when everyone is ush-ered in and assigned a seat by the usher. This is particularly true after the service has begun. This does not mean that the worshiper's choice will not be honored. People usually like to sit in the same general location within the sanctuary. The usher learns this through experience and without difficulty grants the preference.

The question, "Any preference?" should be asked of each visitor. If a preference is expressed, it should be granted as nearly as possible. If no preference is given, the usher uses his discretion in the matter.

The usher's procedure will be determined by whether the person is a regular worshiper or visitor, the size of the aisle, time of seating, number of ushers, and the flow of worshipers.

During the rush period the ushers should work as a team. One should stand down in the aisle at the end of the pew where he wants the worshiper to sit. His greeting in this position must be limited to a smile or nod of recognition. Conversation will be a minimum, as he must quickly move to another pew to seat others. This keeps the usher from having to rush up and down the aisle and at the same time moves the people quickly to a pew. At no time must the usher allow his work to degenerate into herding the people. He is to usher.

Bottlenecks

Each church is likely to have its own peculiar bottlenecks. In some cases it may be the coatracks. If so the usher, whenever possible, should help the older people with their coats and overshoes. Whatever the hindrance may be, if the ushers are aware of it, doubtless they will be able to devise some helpful plans to eliminate congestion. A remodeling change suggested to the building committee might help to eliminate small halls and similar bottlenecks. Portable equipment is sometimes the answer.

SECURING INFORMATION

There are varied methods used in securing the names of visitors.

Visitors' Cards

In some instances the greeter is furnished with a regular visitor's card with a place for name, permanent and city address, telephone, and remarks. A double card with information relative to the church on one card to be kept by the visitor is a good idea. It is not wise to ask for too much information on a visitor's card. For example: If a place is included for church membership, the visitor may write a church of another denomination when in reality he is dissatisfied and is looking for a new church home. An ethical bar-

42

rier may be raised. The church caller or pastor, when furnished the name and address, can call on the person and secure more personal information such as this from him later.

There are several methods of passing out the visitors' cards. The greeter may hand them out as visitors arrive. The pastor may have the visitors stand and have the ushers pass the cards out during the service, or the cards may be placed in the racks on the back of the pews and attention called to them. The latter two methods have distinct disadvantages.

The best method, according to one survey, is to have either the greeter or the visitor fill out the card in the vestibule before entering the sanctuary. Printed instructions on the card will be of help to the visitor if he is expected to fill the card out and place it in the collection plate. When the greeter fills out the card, it often saves time and confusion of illegible writing. This is of particular importance if the pastor plans to use the cards in introducing the visitor during the service. If the name is an unusual one, the greeter might indicate how to pronounce the name correctly. A good procedure is for the host to introduce the guest to the usher, or to give the usher the card, so he will know the visitor's name. The use of the visitor's name is a powerful recognition tool; ushers should school themselves in remembering and using names.

Guest Books

Some churches use registration books. When this method is employed the guest book is usually placed in the vestibule on a special stand or table, and as the visitor enters he writes his name in it. This method has not proved satisfactory for many. It provides a historical record but does not help if the pastor wishes to introduce the visitor in the service unless someone is charged with the responsibility of transferring the information to a card for the pastor.

USING THE INFORMATION

The purpose of securing information is twofold: first, to better welcome the visitor; second, to follow up the contact.

Introductions

Most pastors and laypersons appreciate public and personal recognition of visitors. When this is to be done, the card should be received from the visitor before he enters the sanctuary. The problem is to get the cards into the hands of the pastor. The usher may take them to the pastor as he goes to the front for the offertory prayer. If the cards are received in the offering plates, the head usher may take them from the plates and carry them directly to the pastor or give them to a choir member nearest an accessible door, who will in turn give them to the pastor. When this method is used, the pastor will have the names of all visitors. Then he can call the names and cities of the visitors and have them stand. When this is done in a gracious manner, it creates a bond of friendship.

The pastor, ushers, and other laypersons should make it a point to meet the visitors in a more personal manner after the service. If the visitor is a guest of a member of the congregation, then the chuch member may take the initiative in introducing the visitor to the pastor. If not, the usher or greeter should introduce the visitor to the pastor and to others with whom he will likely have common interests.

Sunday School and Church Visitors

One of the difficult problems is to secure the names of visitors who have also attended Sunday School. Generally they come from the classes with the group, and unless special care is taken they will be overlooked when introductions are made. The Sunday School secretary could prepare a list for the greeter or usher, and a quick check could

be made in order to avoid duplication or omission of someone.

Follow-up Program

In case a follow-up program is used in the church, the
visiting team, Sunday School workers, evangelistic committee, or the pastor should call within the following week. A
personal letter from the pastor expressing appreciation for
having him in the service and welcoming him to return is a
good thing. A mimeographed letter is much less desirable
but better than nothing. Some churches do not have the public introduction of visitors but carry on intensive follow-up
programs.

RECEIVING THE OFFERING

In larger churches a group of collectors are selected to
receive the offering. They are stationed at given locations
within the congregation. Each has a reserved seat. When the
pastor calls for the collectors, they stand for the offertory
prayer and then receive the offering. When the collection is
completed and the money is given to the counters, the collectors return to their assigned places.

In some churches the ushers serve as the collectors. In
that case they usually gather at the rear of the auditorium
and at a given signal march to the front. They either bring the
offering plates with them or receive them from the pastor. If
the aisles are long and it is possible for the ushers to enter
from the side, much time is saved.

The collectors should not be required to serve more
than 8 to 12 rows of pews. If the auditorium has 20 rows of
pews, one set of ushers or collectors could begin at the first
row and another set at the 11th row. Everyone should be
served including the minister, choir, and nursery attendants.

It is never wise to receive the offering from the rear to

the front. The worshiper may feel that he is being assailed from the rear. Of greater importance, the worshiper knows when to expect the plates and has a better opportunity of being prepared with his offering. If the pastor desires to pray a prayer of thanks and consecration over the offering after it is received rather than praying before, it will be worth the extra time involved to have the collectors return to the front. Extra offering plates may be all that is necessary to shorten the time to receive the offering.

Problems

The offering plates should have soft material in the bottom to check the rattle of coins on wooden or aluminum plates. Pencils and envelopes should be provided in the racks on the back of the pews or in the offering plates.

There are several problems such as coming in together, staying together, returning, or leaving the auditorium together. With proper understanding as to what is expected and with instructions from the head usher these can be solved.

Often a person is late in filling out a check or envelope. It is better to indicate that it will be picked up on the return trip rather than hold up all the ushers.

Occasionally the offering plates are upset. When this happens a spare should be passed immediately into the pew, so that the remainder of the offering will not be delayed. The head usher or a spare usher should assist with the offering while the money is being retrieved by the usher who was at the scene.

If two collectors use the same aisle, they should be near the same height. They should walk together in step. Being different heights is not as obvious when they are in two separate aisles.

The offering should be received in a reverent and orderly manner. There should be complete cooperation between the collectors. If the ushers serve as collectors, which is the custom in many churches, care should be taken to have a sufficient number on the job at all times. If at all possible one usher should remain at the entrance of the sanctuary while the offering is being received.

Counters

The money should be kept in a safe place until counted. Some churches use the plan of placing the plates in the pulpit until after the service. If the money is counted during the service, the counters miss much of the benefit of the worship hour. In this case the counters should be rotated.

These counters may be ushers, collectors, or still others selected for this specific task.

It is well for the counters to make several copies of their report, one to keep themselves, one to be placed with the money and given to the treasurer or deposited directly, and one to be given to the pastor. Churches should provide printed forms for listing the money as it is counted.

Money may be listed by source as follows: individual listing of tithe envelopes by number, amount and then totaled, loose offering, building fund, specials, and also other departments like the Sunday School, young people, and missionary society when the church has adopted the Uniform Church Accounting System. The counters should make out the deposit slip, go by the bank immediately after each service, and place the deposit in the bank's night depository chute for prompt protection.

The church is not primarily a financial agency, yet when dealing with finances the Lord and the people expect it to be handled in a businesslike manner.

5 Ushering for Special Occasions

The unforeseen and extraordinary is apt to occur in the special service. It is on these occasions that the extra value of good ushering is appreciated.

SOUL WINNER IN EVANGELISTIC SERVICE

It should be understood that only Christian ushers should attempt soul winning. It is a tremendous job to meet, greet, seat, and prepare the people for the worship service. It is an even greater accomplishment to win a soul to Christ. All the preliminary work of the usher has an indirect bearing on winning souls. On the other hand, more often than not, it requires a direct invitation and effort to lead a needy soul to Christ.

The usher has an advantage over the regular worshiper in opportunities to win others to Christ during the evangelistic service. He meets the people as they enter the church building and knows who is in attendance. He knows where they are seated. In fact, he can have a part in seating them to an advantage for altar work. To do this, the usher should know the person. In a few cases a person will react better to the invitation if he is seated in the rear of the church, but generally speaking the sinner should be seated near the middle or to the front section of the congregation. If possible it is well to seat him near the end of a pew. This makes it easier for him to step to the aisle and to the altar.

The usher has free access to the aisles, and he can move about during the invitation in order to extend a personal invitation to the spiritually needy. His movements are likely to be less conspicuous than those of others. He has the additional advantage of having met the worshiper before the service. As he meets him to extend the invitation to receive Christ, it is like meeting a friend or previous acquaintance.

To be a successful soul winner the usher must think of himself in that light and work toward that end. He would do well to study a book on altar work or attend training classes on doing altar work effectively.

The usher's interest in an individual, his zeal and passion for his salvation, and his manner of approach are dominant factors in leading a person to Christ. In the event the person does not understand what is meant by being born again or does not understand the purpose of the altar, the usher may tell him that the altar is a good place for him to pray and confess his sins and his need of Christ. He should assure the needy one that to kneel will not be a point of embarrassment but a joy to all the church.

In many cases the soul winner should explain that going to the altar is not an act of joining the church. Upon occasions the usher may deem it advisable to walk with the seeker to the altar. At least the soul winner usher could tell of the time he knelt at an altar and that God met his need.

The usher who in loving interest gives a short, scriptural, positive, personal invitation and keeps to the primary issue of having the seeker kneel and pray for a definite need is likely to be an effectual soul winner.

There are times during the general altar call given by the minister when the usher can be of inestimable help. He may be asked by the pastor to stand at the front and direct persons to the altar. He can secure extra chairs for seekers when the altar is filled. Some churches have extensions that the ushers add to the altar as it fills.

The usher should also check the ventilation as it is related to the altar. Generally, with a number of seekers and Christian workers gathered around the altar, there is need for cross-room ventilation.

When an evangelist is making an invitation to the congregation the pastor often directs the seekers to the place of prayer. The wise usher will be sensitive to his responsibility in this regard and cooperate with the pastor when and where needed.

Norman Oke has suggested in his book *We Have an Altar* that an usher may post a sign: "Quiet, Please, During the Altar Service." This sign along with the example of the ushers near the exit should tend to discourage loud conversation and distracting disturbances while there are seekers at the altar. The usher would not be out of place to check children who thoughtlessly run and play in the church during the altar service.

The invitation to the altar and the time of prayer at the altar is the climactic moment of the evangelistic efforts of pastor, evangelist, congregation, and the blessings of the Holy Spirit combined. Great events and lasting decisions are made. Dignity and Christian consideration should characterize this part of the service. The usher can contribute much to the atmosphere by his example.

After the Altar Service

All too often the person who has found Christ at an altar of prayer leaves the altar and the church without many people giving an encouraging handshake. If the usher will take the time to speak to the happy new Christian and give words of appreciation and encouragement, it will mean much. This is the time when the individual is most receptive to friendly understanding and advice.

To meet the person who refused the invitation to the altar is equally important. The individual may have misunderstood or been somewhat embarrassed by having someone talk to him. If the usher will take a little time after the service to assure the one who rejected his invitation that he is still interested in him and will pray for him, perhaps the door for future opportunities will be left open. Many pastors and personal workers testify to the fact that often those who reject the invitation during the actual altar call yield to a second invitation while the altar service is in progress. To say the least, an expressed interest and a cheerful good-bye help the needy person to leave the church knowing that there are those who are genuinely interested in him.

HOST AT BAPTISMAL SERVICE

The occasional baptismal service is freighted with hazards. When a congregation becomes accustomed to a baptismal service each week, the likelihood of confusion diminishes. In churches where a baptismal service is conducted only once a quarter or annually, the usher's responsibility is increasingly apparent.

The baptismal service should be sacred, beautiful, and meaningful. There are grave dangers when the immersion method is used at a lake, river, or seashore. If children are allowed to make it an occasion for play, if robes are used, or if blunders are made in the ritual, the possibilities for laughter, immodesty, confusion, and disturbance are great. On these occasions the usher's usefulness is seen partly in how he reacts to save a bad situation. His full value, though not obvious, is proved in how successful he is in keeping emergencies from arising.

The place of the baptismal service determines what equipment is needed. When the service is in the church the usher's task is much easier. If the service is held in a church other than his own, the usher should familiarize himself with the general plan of the church, the specific needs relative to the candidates, baptismal entrance and exit, and his definite responsibility in the procedure of the service.

If the service is held by a river, lake, or ocean, the need for the usher's assistance is greater. If a committee has not been appointed to provide a tent or other suitable facilities for the candidates' use in dressing, the usher should attend to this. If the weather is warm and the candidates plan to return home before redressing the usher could group three or four cars to provide a degree of privacy while the candidates wait. The tents or car groups, for both men and women, should be placed in such a manner as to assure privacy. A handrail should be installed along steep banks leading into the water. If this cannot be arranged, the usher should be near to give the needed assistance. Songbooks, portable organs, and the other like items are a help in the service. The usher should have them available.

If a river or lake is used, the usher should assist the worshipers in finding the route to the location. Generally, these should be well known to all, but occasionally a location is chosen where an unfamiliar turn must be made in order to reach the location. A sign or an usher posted at such a place would be a help to those who might otherwise miss the turn and the service.

Parking the cars can be a cause of confusion. An usher or two can solve this problem with a little foresight. It is obvious that when cars are properly parked a greater number can occupy the same amount of space, and the convenience in leaving the location is increased.

People generally stand during these outdoor services. The usher should direct them to the general area for an advantageous view. The song leader can lead the singing more effectively if the group is compact.

The usher should check the safety of the waterfront in advance of the service. He should take it as part of his duty to point out the dangerous areas. Parents should keep small children near them, but if they fail to do this, the usher should take charge. The outside setting is an invitation to many to play with rocks, twigs, and in the water. For the safety of the people and the sanctity of the service, the usher may be forced to take firm action at times.

HELPER AT COMMUNION SERVICE

The Communion service is unlike the baptismal service in that it is not accompanied with hilarious emergencies. The usher's contribution to worship in the Communion service is seen in his ability to cooperate with the pastor and other elders serving the elements. In addition to his regular duties he has the task of seating the worshipers so that the Communion tray can pass from person to person. If Communion is served at the altar, he should direct the worshipers to the Communion rail so as to eliminate overcrowding. All too often the worshipers are allowed to flock to the Communion table, and those who do not find space at the Communion altar are left to mill around in the front of the sanctuary. A proper plan executed with the cooperation of the people will solve this problem.

At the Pews

When Communion is served to the worshiper while he is seated in the pew, the ushers are not as involved. The elders or stewards generally have the responsibility of serving the Communion. If the usher is used, there are several items of importance that he should know. He should know how many each tray will serve. He should be assigned only as

53

many pews as a tray will serve. His station as related to others should be clearly defined. He should be briefed on the procedure of the service, particularly if it should be his first time to serve.

At the Altar

Where Communion is served only once each quarter, the value of meeting at the altar far outweighs the extra time involved. With an adequate corps of ushers and definite procedure of service, several hundred can be served in a short time. Each church differs from the next as to the number of sections, position of choir, entrances, exits, balcony, and aisles. The usher should have a clear understanding as to what is expected of him and then follow through according to instructions.

Let us take an example of a small church with two sections of pews and with an altar where 20 may be served. We will suppose that the choir has 14 persons in it including the pianist and director. There are 60 people in the auditorium's two sections. The one to the right of the pastor as he stands behind the pulpit we will call Section A; and the one to his left, Section B. There are three aisles. Beginning with the one to the pastor's right, we will number them aisle 1, 2 and 3, with number 2 being in the center.

Ushers A-1 and A-2 will serve Section A, while ushers B-1 and B-2 will serve Section B. Ushers B-1 and B-2 will work out of aisle 3. When the pastor invites the first table, ushers A-1 and A-2 will signal the worshipers in Section A to stand, and those desiring to take Communion will move to their left into aisle 1. Usher A-1 will lead them to the front and across in front of the altar. Usher A-2 counts each communicant as he leaves the pew, and when 20 (the number necessary to fill the altar) persons enter the aisle, he will ask the remaining ones to be seated and wait for a later table. The advantage in having everyone stand is that those who do not desire Communion will permit the others to pass them freely. Ushers A-1 and A-2 will sit on the front pew and await the completion of the serving of the first table. When the minister asks the communicants to arise, ushers A-2 and A-1 will lead the people back to their respective pews. Note that usher A-2 leads back and A-1 follows.

As they return, ushers B-1 and B-2 should have the worshipers in Section B stand, and those desiring Communion move to aisle 3 and follow usher B-1 to the altar. Usher B-2 counts 20 persons and then asks the others to remain at their seats. Thus one group leaves the table as others come. When those in the auditorium have been served, then those in the choir along with the pianist and director may be served. The procedure of ushering will depend upon the entrance and exit to the choir rostrum. Occasionally there are those who cannot kneel at the altar. In such an instance it is proper to seat the worshiper on the front pew. An adapted plan will work smoothly in any church with one or more tables to be served.

In a larger church one corps of ushers working with the pastor regularly leads 600 to 800 communicants to the Communion altar, where they are served, and then leads them back to their pews. The altar will accommodate 50; thus up to 16 servings are required. They have their program so perfected that the serving is completed in a gracious manner in only 30 minutes.

The pastor stands behind the pulpit and eight elders assist him. Two elders serve the table and exchange empty trays for full ones with the stewards who work in the preparation room. Three elders serve the bread and three the cup. Each has one-third section of the altar that he serves; and when he has completed his section, he returns to his position. The main problem is to move the people to and from the altar.

The church auditorium has three sections of pews and a U-shaped balcony. There are two ushers assigned to each section of pews and four to the balcony. The ushers are so situated that one in each pair leads the group back to the pews as the other usher follows. Thus two ushers from the east lead 50 persons to the altar, and as they lead them back, the two ushers from the west side lead 50 persons to the altar. The alert ushers alternate the groups from east to west to center with never a moment lost. The confusion of one group running into another is eliminated. The efficiency of the ushering adds to the sacredness of the occasion, and everyone welcomes the opportunity of participating in Communion at the altar.

Securing Cooperation

The people must cooperate with the ushers in whatever plan is used to serve Communion. When an excellent method is adopted, the habit pattern of the people will assist the usher.

Before the habit pattern is established, the pastor can do much by way of announcements. The announcements may be verbal, printed in the bulletin, or both. They should be specific and clearly stated in order to achieve best results. One pastor placed the following in his bulletin:

Instructions to Communicants: Follow instructions of ushers. Each table will partake as a group on indication by pastor. After receiving sacraments, place cup on altar rail and rise with group on signal from pastor. The group will then follow usher back to their respective seats. May we all be in an attitude of prayer as we partake of the sacraments in remembrance of Him.

OTHER SERVICES

There are many gatherings held in a church that may or may not require the services of the regular church usher. On occasions when his services are not required the head usher at least could share his knowledge of the sanctuary and equipment with those in charge.

The Wedding

In the majority of church weddings the ushers will be selected by the bride. In case the regular ushers are to be used, a meeting of the head usher and the person in charge of the wedding arrangements several days before the wedding is a necessity. Details as to dress, reserved section, special guest identification, and other important details should be agreed upon. The usher should remember that the desire of the bride, or her appointed assistant, is final as to procedure.

The Funeral

The question "Who is in charge?" may determine the procedure of ushering at a funeral. Generally the undertaker and his assistants are best qualified. But again the regular ushers should lend every assistance possible. The occasion determines that ushering be more formal at a funeral, and the usher should bear himself accordingly.

Rallies, Assemblies, and Conventions

All too often at these special short-time, mass gatherings church ushering is at its poorest level. Unless specific arrangements are made in advance, the staff of ushers of the local church is in charge. If the local staff is not sufficient, the head usher could secure a number of ushers from a neighboring church to assist.

Generally the special-type service is characterized by having numerous visitors and friends. If special attention is not given to ushering, the very ones who need help and attention will not receive it. In these services the ushers of the host church have an added responsibility to those who are strangers in their midst. Unless they sense the responsibility no one will, and the friends and visitors will be left to shift for themselves.

Several points to watch at mass gatherings are:

1. Have sufficient ushers and offering plates to serve the group quickly. For extra large crowds, plastic cartons may be used. It is best to have one for each row.

2. Since many who attend wish to visit with acquaintances of former days, they are likely to congregate in the aisles and cause congestion. Keep aisles clear.

3. If all the pews are filled, the overflow rooms should be opened, and extra chairs should be readily available. These should be placed so as not to be a hazard in case of fire or other emergencies.

4. Extra chairs for platform guests should be provided.

5. Special and more frequent attention should be given to air conditioning and heating in mass meetings.

6. By and large, special attention should be given to every phase of church ushering in terms of a larger attendance.

Special Meetings

Where thousands are expected, the traffic flow, auto parking, rest room facilities, first aid station, phone availability, and many other details should be familiar to the ushers.

6 Organization and Tools

ORGANIZATION

The organization of the corps of ushers is the responsibility of the church board. The usual practice is for the pastor to recommend a person for head usher to the church board for appointment. Thus the head usher is responsible to the pastor and the board.

Officers

The head usher is chairman of the board of ushers. It is generally his responsibility, with the approval of the pastor, to appoint the other ushers. It would be well to select an assistant head usher to take over when the head usher must be absent. Other officers may be selected as the need demands.

Meetings

The training program is discussed in another chapter. However, definite times should be set for meetings. The least number would be twice a year, and once each month would not be too often in larger churches. An inspirational program along with a training course gives esprit de corps to the ushers. Occasionally the pastor or an outside speaker should address the group on such subjects as calling, commitment, and contribution.

Assignments

The head usher with the approval of the pastor should work out assignments. The assignments should not be left entirely to the individual usher's choice since the head usher and pastor have a more objective view of the need. With an experienced corps of ushers the duties are rotated.

THE USHER'S TOOLS

Checklist

Many ushers will do their task without a written checklist, but as a safeguard against omitting even one of the specific duties a memo checklist would be helpful. The following list is suggestive of the usual. If a checklist similar to the one below is used, space should be provided for special needs under each heading. These special needs may occur only occasionally, but they are obvious to the congregation if not cared for:

Usher's Checklist

Sunday _____ A.M. _____ P.M. _____, 19____

A. Workers
   1. Greeters _____ Collectors _____
   2. Ushers _____
   3. All at stations with necessary materials _____
   4. Appearance of workers _____
   5. Identification badges (or flowers) _____
   6. Consult pastor as to the special needs _____
   7. Special items _____
B. Building
   1. Sidewalks clean and safe _____
   2. Doors opened _____
   3. Ventilation correct _____ Lights on _____
   4. Loudspeakers adjusted _____

5. Organ and piano opened _____
6. Nursery ready _____
7. Phone available _____
8. Special items _____

C. Materials
1. Change or soften phone ring _____
2. Hearing aids available _____
3. Hymnals and bulletins ready _____
4. Visitors' cards _____ Pencils _____
5. Collection plates _____ Offering envelopes _____
6. Flowers in place _____
7. Special items _____

The above is only a tentative list. Careful study will reveal the needs in a local situation. The advantage of a checklist is that a comprehensive survey of the needs is made each week, and a systematic method of procedure is adopted.

In addition to following the checklist, the usher must be prepared for the unexpected problems. He should imagine certain emergencies and then think through what he would do under similar circumstances.

1. What would he do in case of fire?

2. Could he help direct worshipers out in an orderly fashion?

3. What would he do if someone took property from the vestibule?

4. What would he do if an intruder disturbed the service?

5. What would he do in case of a storm or if the lights went out?

The usher should be one that can be depended upon in case of emergencies.

Supplies

There are certain materials that assist the usher in eliminating disturbances. There should be an assigned space where the ushers may keep supplies and materials, just as there is a caretaker's closet. Among the supplies he should have are the following items:

Dustcloth, sponge, and *small pan.* A small child was sick and lost his previous meal during a service. His mother was unable to get him out of the sanctuary quickly enough. An alert usher, with the use of cleaning materials, soon took care of the situation.

Cleaning tissues. These have so many uses that a generous supply in the usher's cabinet is wise. A box of them should be kept in the pulpit. There are times when seekers at the altar need them.

Smelling salts. Occasionally someone faints during a service. A bottle of smelling salts or some similar product should be available.

Soft toys. Many churches are providing a nursery for small children. However, those who want their children with them in the sanctuary sometimes allow the children to play with keys, coins, or metal toys. The noise is distracting, and damage can be done to the furnishings. If the usher has access to soft toys and could courteously present one to the parent for the child's use during the service, it might eliminate the noise and at the same time serve as a mild reminder of the disturbing conditions.

First-aid kit, pins, thread, and other such items. One secret of the usher's usefulness is in being prepared for any emergency.

Signals

The ushers, in cooperation with the pastor, should work out a system of signals. A number of churches use a buzzer system to call in the choir at the appropriate moment. If this is not feasible the pastor can signal the usher, and he can relay the message to the waiting choir.

Other churches have an intercom system whereby the pastor attracts the attention of the head usher by means of a flashing light or telephone.

The great majority of churches are small enough not to warrant so elaborate a system. Yet the pastor and head usher should have signals for routine communications. An usher in the rear was heard to call out to one near the front. "We have two more. Can you seat them?" The people felt conspicuous as the unthoughtful members of the congregation turned around to see who was entering.

One of the most common signals used by ushers is to hold up a number of fingers, against the background of the usher's suit, to indicate the number of seats available or the number of persons to be seated. Other common signals used between ushers to relay information are as follows:

1. Hand held up with palm toward observer, to indicate every seat taken.

2. Hand cupped over ear to indicate the need of hearing aid.

3. Hand held up with fingers turned down to indicate that worshiper desires to be seated about halfway in the auditorium.

4. Closed fist, to indicate a desire on the part of the worshiper to be seated near the front.

The ushers should work out simple signals to meet their needs. For church services the hand signals are more suitable than arm-waving signals.

CONCLUSION

Thus by careful preparation and performance, ushering in the church becomes a great ministry. The annals of God in the day of judgment will no doubt reveal the ministry of ushering assisted in the salvation of souls; and the Christian usher will hear, "Well done, good and faithful servant; thou hast been faithful over a few things, I will make thee ruler over many things . . ." (Matt. 25:23).